Just as we give, we must also be open to accepting the gifts of others. In Jesus, God gives us the most precious gift of all and invites us to know and follow his only Son. Whatever your Christmas looks like, everyone is invited to the birth of Jesus.

wealthy Magi, all

and d

You too are welcon

and find yourself in t

you are known ar

We hope that you have a blessed Christmas and pray that your journey following the star leads you ever closer to the joy and peace of knowing Jesus Christ.

Archbishop Justin Welby   **Archbishop John Sentamu**

God of wonder,
as we follow the star,
open our minds
to search for you,
open our eyes to see you,
and open our hearts
to receive your love,
this Christmas and always.

Amen.

12 Days of Christmas Wonder

How to use this booklet

'We Three Kings' is an incredibly well-known carol written from the perspective of the wise men (or Magi) as they follow the star to discover Jesus.

This year's reflections invite us to go on a similar journey of wonder and discovery, using daily themes suggested by the words of the carol's chorus:

O star of wonder, star of night,
star with royal beauty bright,
westward leading,
still proceeding,
guide us to thy perfect light.
John Henry Hopkins (1820–1891)

There are reflections for each of the 12 days of Christmas, starting with Christmas Day and ending on 5 January. (The Feast of the Epiphany is normally celebrated on 6 January, but in 2020 many churches will mark it on 5 January which falls on a Sunday.)

As well as the reflections, each day offers a practical challenge to bring the theme alive together with a short prayer. There is always a slightly longer suggested Bible passage to read if you want to go a bit deeper.

When Epiphany arrives and the wise men finally reach their destination, maybe you will have made some discoveries of your own about your journey of faith and the gifts you bring along the way.

Sharing the journey with children

'We Three Kings' is as well-known to children as it is to adults and there is plenty of scope to use the reflections with children. The introductions, challenges and prayers have been written to be accessible to all ages.

There are also accompanying craft activities designed to help families explore the daily themes. See overleaf for details of how to access these.

Other ways to join the journey

The free *Follow The Star* app – available for Android and iOS devices – allows anyone to join the journey. As well as the complete text of the booklet, the app also includes full audio for each day, including the Bible reading, the daily craft activities and a guide to Christmas and Epiphany services near you.

Alternatively, anyone can sign up for free e-mail versions of the reflections via **www.churchofengland.org/followthestar** where you will also find links to the family craft activities, videos and much more.

Social media is also a great way to join and share the journey. Make sure you're following The Church of England and look out for daily #FollowTheStar posts from Advent right through to Epiphany.

Star

We all have questions: big ones and small ones. Some questions, though, might change the course of our lives when we search for the answers.

Read Matthew 2.1–8

In the time of King Herod, after Jesus was born in Bethlehem of Judea, wise men from the East came to Jerusalem asking, 'Where is the child who has been born king of the Jews? For we observed his star at its rising and have come to pay him homage.'

Curiosity is a powerful thing. The urge to find out more can lead us in all sorts of directions and it certainly leads the wise men to leave their homes and journey towards an unknown place, following only an unusual star. The wise men have noticed that something is out of the ordinary, something that pulls them, something they can't ignore.

Today, on Christmas Day, we celebrate the birth of Jesus. He is the promised king, the child the wise men eventually find and worship. But they're not there yet. For now, they're still on the journey. They still have questions. They're still searching but they know that what they find will be worth it.

CHALLENGE

Where are you on your journey with God? What questions do you have about Jesus?
Write down your questions and your thoughts and see what answers you find through the next few days.

PRAYER

God of surprises, we bring our questions to you. Show us more about Jesus as we travel through the coming days. Amen.

Wonder

There are so many things in the world we can't quite explain or which take our breath away. And when we find something amazing it can be hard to stop ourselves trying to find out more.

Read Psalm 65.6–13

Those who live at earth's farthest bounds are awed by your signs; you make the gateways of the morning and the evening shout for joy. You visit the earth and water it, you greatly enrich it; the river of God is full of water; you provide the people with grain, for so you have prepared it.

There's no doubt that the universe is an amazing place. There are trillions of stars out there and each one is a small miracle of gas and gravity. Looking at the stars in the night sky tells a story that started millions of years ago. Only now do we see the light that started its journey back before most of our ancestors were born.

Every star is incredible, and yet the wise men, looking up, had to wonder what they were seeing. These men who studied the skies and who knew the stars inside out could still be amazed. In the midst of God's spectacular creation, something unusual called to them and opened their minds to look in awe.

CHALLENGE

Stand outside and look into the night sky.
What amazes you? What is it about the world God created that makes you wonder?

PRAYER

Father, we thank you for the things you have made that amaze us. Help us to keep looking in wonder. Amen.

Night

Night time can be scary. It's hard to see, and there is always the fear of what might be hiding in the dark. Eventually, though, dawn will come and a new day will begin.

Read Luke 1.68–79

"By the tender mercy of our God,
the dawn from on high will break upon us,
to give light to those who sit in darkness
and in the shadow of death,
to guide our feet into the way of peace."

Jesus is born into a community which is waiting for a saviour to come. At the time of Jesus' birth, the Jewish people had been living under the control of the Romans. They needed to believe that one day things would be different, that hope was on its way.

A star, shining brightly in the sky, points towards a baby who is born to be light in the darkness. This baby is going to bring a new day to end the night of fear and worry and oppression. The darkness of war and struggle and pain is about to be consumed by dawning light. God has not forgotten his people. Light and life is breaking through.

CHALLENGE

Where do you see light dawning in dark situations? Watch or read the news. Ask for God to bring light and hope to one of the situations you learn about.

PRAYER

Thank you, God, that with you there is always hope. Bring your light to the dark situations we face in our world. Amen.

Royal

Sometimes it feels as if pain and hardship are the way of the world and there is nothing we can do to change the situation. Systems, though, can be overturned by unexpected people.

Read Revelation 21.1–7

"See, the home of God is among mortals...
God himself will be with them; he will wipe every tear from their eyes. Death will be no more; mourning and crying and pain will be no more, for the first things have passed away."

The wise men have come looking for a king and Herod is worried. He knows that this child they speak of is a threat to his authority and he has to do something. Somehow he has to take this special child out of the picture and death is the surest way to stop a new king rising.

Today the Church remembers 'The Holy Innocents' – the infant boys Herod orders to be killed as he attempts to track down Jesus. As mothers shed tears for their murdered children, a king is coming who will turn Herod's old order upside down. The child Herod seeks will bring in a kingdom where every tear will be wiped away and death and pain will be banished for ever.

CHALLENGE

Do you know someone who is grieving? What is painful for you to see or hear?
Bring these things to God and watch for signs of healing and comfort today.

PRAYER

Father, we bring to you our pain and our sadness. Wipe away our tears and fill us with hope. Amen.

Beauty

Whatever our definition of beauty, we can probably agree that if something is beautiful it 'sticks out' from what is around it. We see it or sense it, and we find it hard to resist.

Read Psalm 19.1–6

The heavens are telling the glory of God; and the firmament proclaims his handiwork... There is no speech, nor are there words; their voice is not heard; yet their voice goes out through all the earth, and their words to the end of the world.

Everyone's definition of beauty is different. Artists paint it. Musicians compose music that somehow captures it. Hearts and emotions respond to it. For some it is about what we see on the outside. For others it is about an experience that brings joy.

Whatever beauty is, it is captivating, and the wise men cannot resist the natural beauty they see in the night sky. They are drawn to the star, the work of God's hand, and they have to follow. They have to find out more. The outward beauty and mystery of the star is about to lead them to the most beautiful gift they could ever imagine: a child who will light up the whole world.

CHALLENGE

Take a photo of something beautiful you see today. Share it via message or social media and tell people about the beauty you've seen.

PRAYER

God of beauty, thank you for all that you have created. Help us to celebrate the special things we see today. Amen.

Bright

It's sometimes hard to name our own best qualities. Often, it's easier for those around us to see what brightness we bring to the world.

Read Psalm 139.13–16

For it was you who formed my inward parts;
you knit me together in my mother's womb.
I praise you,
for I am fearfully and wonderfully made.
Wonderful are your works;
that I know very well.

Even now, no one knows for sure what the Star of Bethlehem actually was. Some say it was a comet. Some say it was the light that comes from a new star being born. Whatever the truth is, we do know that there was something out of the ordinary about what the wise men saw. Just like this special star, God has made each one of us uniquely and wonderfully.

We are one of a kind too. God knows us fully and, like the star, has given us our own distinctive shining qualities to help to make the world around us a brighter place: compassion, love, an infectious sense of joy, peace, patience, kindness, loyalty, a quest for fairness.

What are your shining qualities? What brightness do you bring and how will you shine today?

CHALLENGE

Use a whiteboard marker to write your shining qualities on a mirror. When you look in the mirror, remember that God made you in a wonderful way to bring brightness to the world.

PRAYER

Lord Jesus, help me to use what you have given me to make the world a brighter place today. Amen.

Leading

New Year's resolutions give us hope and direction, but keeping them is not always easy. If we're not careful, we can find ourselves quickly getting off track.

Read Isaiah 43.18–21

I am about to do a new thing;
now it springs forth, do you not perceive it?
I will make a way in the wilderness
and rivers in the desert.

God is doing something new. God has sent his Son to bring hope and light and life to a world where his people are oppressed and kept down. The wise men sense this exciting "newness" and want to be part of it. They follow the lead of the star, wherever it takes them, because they have committed themselves to finding the new king. They have a hope that leads them on, and they show perseverance when the journey takes time and effort.

At this time of year, we also experience this sense of hope and "newness". Unfortunately, research suggests that less than a quarter of us who make New Year's resolutions will actually keep them. While there's something attractive about taking new directions in life, it takes courage to stick to the course.

CHALLENGE

Where do you want to go this year? What hope or desire is leading you? Write down a New Year's resolution you want to try to keep.

PRAYER

Father God, lead us towards the new things you want in our lives. Help us to keep going when the way gets hard. Amen.

Day 8 New Year's Day

Proceeding

Some journeys can be difficult, or even dangerous. Knowing that there is someone along for the ride with you, to help you and to be beside you can really make a difference.

Read Psalm 23

The Lord is my shepherd, I shall not want…
Even though I walk through the darkest valley,
I fear no evil;
for you are with me;
your rod and your staff – they comfort me.

For many people, travelling companions are an essential part of any journey. They are there to share the ups and downs, the joyful moments and the tougher times. We don't know exactly how many wise men are following the star, but we know that there is more than one of them along for the ride! The journey is a long one and there are obstacles to meet on the way, including a jealous and two-faced king.

As Herod plots murder, the wise men discover that they have an unexpected traveller alongside them. God warns them in a dream not to go back to Herod when they have found the child. Through adventure and through danger, God is with the wise men and will make sure they stay on the right path.

CHALLENGE

Who is with you on your journey? Think of someone who supports or cares for you and send them a message or phone them to say thank you.

PRAYER

Thank you, God, that wherever we go and whatever we face you are with us. Keep us safe on our journey through life. Amen.

Guide

In an age of satnav and internet maps, it's rare that we need to stop and ask someone for directions. Sometimes, though, a person is exactly what we need to guide the way.

Read John 14.1–7

Jesus said… "I am the way, and the truth, and the life. No one comes to the Father except through me. If you know me, you will know my Father also. From now on you do know him and have seen him."

23

Stars have been used as navigation tools since ancient times, lighting the sky and showing the way. Even today, the North Star is a guide for wandering nighttime explorers, giving an unwavering direction in the darkness. The wise men are looking up to their own star for guidance and, as it moves, they are assured of the path they follow.

In life, the need for a guide through unfamiliar territory and situations is often very real, whoever and wherever we are. We want the reassurance that we are walking the right way. The child born in Bethlehem, under the sign of the star, will grow to be a guide to millions across the world. He will light the path that leads the way to God.

CHALLENGE

Where do you need direction in life?

Download a finger labyrinth* and follow the pathway with your finger. Ask God to give you the guidance you need.

PRAYER

Loving God, show us the way when we are lost and need direction. Guide us as we journey forward. Amen.

* A template can be downloaded via www.churchofengland.org/followthestar

Light

Darkness has many overwhelming forms: despair, fear, violence, danger, grief, ignorance, worry. Yet some believe that there is one source of light to combat them all.

Read John 8.12–16

Again Jesus spoke to them, saying, "I am the light of the world. Whoever follows me will never walk in darkness but will have the light of life."

Light reveals the dangers covered by darkness. In the light, secrets are revealed and fears are banished. In the light we can see the truth because there is no place to hide. In the light we see beauty in its fullness.

The star's light has been leading the wise men towards the child. When this child grows up, he will call himself the 'light of the world.' He will be the living embodiment of light. He will be the one who highlights dangers, banishes fears, reveals beauty and shows the truth. Jesus will tell us that we no longer have to be afraid, we no longer need to walk in darkness. Jesus will open our eyes to what life can be.

CHALLENGE

What are you trying to understand at the moment? What do you need to see more clearly? Light a candle and ask Jesus to illuminate the situation.

PRAYER

Loving God, show us what is hidden, chase away our fears and give us courage when we are afraid. Amen.

Gifts

Often, the best gifts that we have ever received are the small and personal ones, handmade with love and effort, but costing very little money.

Read Matthew 2.7–12

When they saw that the star had stopped, they were overwhelmed with joy. On entering the house, they saw the child with Mary his mother; and they knelt down and paid him homage. Then, opening their treasure-chests, they offered him gifts of gold, frankincense, and myrrh.

The wise men are carrying precious gifts with them on their journey: gifts that will speak into the story of Jesus' life. Gold is a gift of richness, fit for a king. Myrrh is a precious oil, used to anoint the dead, reminding us of the death Jesus will endure on the cross. Frankincense is an incense used in worship, fitting for a holy child.

But treasures are not always physical. Gifts cannot always be touched. Each of us has gifts and talents within us and each of us can make an offering of our own. Our gifts are part of our own story in our work, our homes and our communities. Our gifts show who we are and what we bring to the world around us.

CHALLENGE

What gifts do you have that you could offer to your friends, your family, your church or your community? Write down one gift you can offer and who you will offer it to.

PRAYER

Generous God, help us to use our gifts in an open-hearted way so that others will know that they are loved and valued. Amen.

Discovery

$\int$ earching for something takes energy and commitment. When you find what you are looking for, there is an understandable urge to celebrate and share your discovery.

Read Luke 11.9–13

Jesus said to his disciples, "So I say to you, Ask, and it will be given to you; search, and you will find; knock, and the door will be opened for you."

At last the wise men reach their journey's end and lay their gifts before the Christ child. They have travelled a great distance from where they started, and they have experienced much along the road. In some ways, though, this is only the beginning.

Sometimes when we find what we think we're looking for, we realize that there is so much more to discover, so many more questions to ask. God understands our curiosity and he welcomes it. God wants us to wonder. God wants us to search. And when we do, he will not hide from us. Just as the star shines brightly to light the way. God's love beckons us forward, inviting us to know him more, step by step by step.

CHALLENGE

Look at the questions you asked at the beginning of this 12-day journey. Have you found any answers? Is there anything you are still searching for?

PRAYER

God of wonder, help us to keep searching, keep asking and keep discovering as we continue on our journey to you. Amen.

Exploring further

We hope you have enjoyed this year's **#FollowTheStar** journey. Here are some ways you might want to travel further in faith in the days and months ahead:

Join others in celebrating the arrival of the wise men

Going to church to celebrate Epiphany is a wonderful way to complete your Christmas journey. Many churches and cathedrals host special carol services to mark the Epiphany season, which lasts up to and including 2 February, the feast of Candlemas.

You can find Epiphany services near you at www.AChurchNearYou.com

Explore God in everyday life with #EverydayFaith

#EverydayFaith is a new campaign from the Church of England which offers 21 days of stories, reflections and prayers to help you find God in everyday life.

Find out more and join in via
www.churchofengland.org/everydayfaith

Sign up for the Church of England's Lent campaign

Join millions of Christians worldwide in marking the 40 days before Easter, beginning on Ash Wednesday which falls on 26 February 2020.

The focus of this year's Church of England campaign will be God's creation and will include a daily challenge to live in a more just and sustainable way.

Find out more and join in via
www.churchofengland.org/lent